2022
Unicorn
coloring
calendar

Want free goodies?

Email us at

◈ nanyandfriends@gmail.com ◈

Title the email "Title book"

And let us know that you purchased

____

This book Belong to..

____

01 JANUARY

sunday	monday	tuesday	wednesday	Thursday	Friday	saturday
						1
2	3	4	5	6	7	8
9	10	11	12	13	14	15
16	17	18	19	20	21	22
23 / 30	24 / 31	25	26	27	28	29

02 FEBRUARY

sunday	monday	tuesday	wednesday	thursday	friday	saturday
		1	2	3	4	5
6	7	8	9	10	11	12
13	14	15	16	17	18	19
20	21	22	23	24	25	26
27	28					

03 MARCH

sunday	monday	tuesday	wednesday	thursday	friday	saturday
		1	2	3	4	5
6	7	8	9	10	11	12
13	14	15	16	17	18	19
20	21	22	23	24	25	26
27	28	29	30	31		

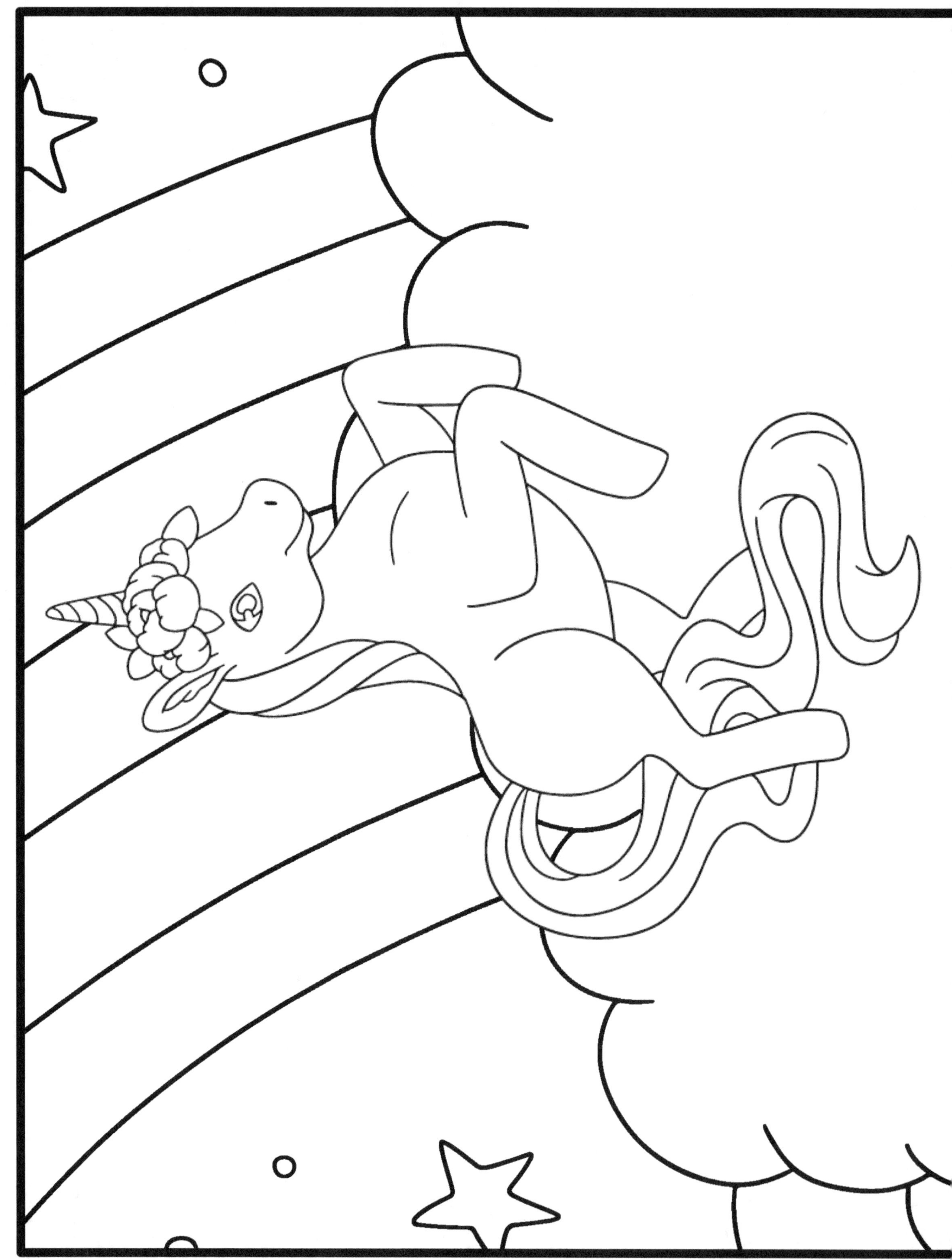

04   APRIL

sunday	monday	tuesday	wednesday	thursday	Friday	saturday
					1	2
3	4	5	6	7	8	9
10	11	12	13	14	15	16
17	18	19	20	21	22	23
24	25	26	27	28	29	30

05 MAY

sunday	monday	tuesday	wednesday	thursday	friday	saturday
1	2	3	4	5	6	7
8	9	10	11	12	13	14
15	16	17	18	19	20	21
22	23	24	25	26	27	28
29	30	31				

06　JUNE

sunday	monday	tuesday	wednesday	thursday	Friday	saturday
			1	2	3	4
5	6	7	8	9	10	11
12	13	14	15	16	17	18
19	20	21	22	23	24	25
26	27	28	29	30		

JULY

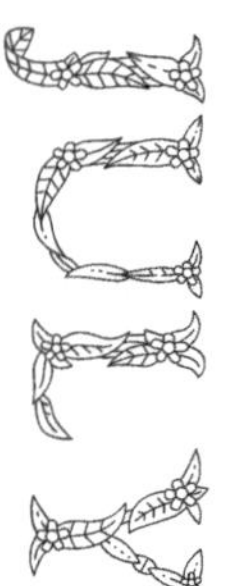

Sunday	Monday	Tuesday	Wednesday	Thursday	Friday	Saturday
					1	2
3	4	5	6	7	8	9
10	11	12	13	14	15	16
17	18	19	20	21	22	23
24	25	26	27	28	29	30
31						

08 AUGUST

sunday	monday	tuesday	wednesday	thursday	friday	saturday
	1	2	3	4	5	6
7	8	9	10	11	12	13
14	15	16	17	18	19	20
21	22	23	24	25	26	27
28	29	30	31			

09 SEPTEMBER

sunday	monday	tuesday	wednesday	thursday	friday	saturday
				1	2	3
4	5	6	7	8	9	10
11	12	13	14	15	16	17
18	19	20	21	22	23	24
25	26	27	28	29	30	

10 OCTOBER

sunday	monday	tuesday	wednesday	thursday	friday	saturday
						1
2	3	4	5	6	7	8
9	10	11	12	13	14	15
16	17	18	19	20	21	22
23	24	25	26	27	28	29
30	31					

11 NOVEMBER

sunday	monday	tuesday	wednesday	thursday	friday	saturday
		1	2	3	4	5
6	7	8	9	10	11	12
13	14	15	16	17	18	19
20	21	22	23	24	25	26
27	28	29	30			

12 DECEMBER

sunday	monday	tuesday	wednesday	thursday	Friday	saturday
				1	2	3
4	5	6	7	8	9	10
11	12	13	14	15	16	17
18	19	20	21	22	23	24
25	26	27	28	29	30	31